Betrayal by a Father and the Power of Forgiveness

BETRAYAL
BY A FATHER
and the POWER
OF FORGIVENESS

Rosibel N. Hernandez

XULON PRESS

Xulon Press
2301 Lucien Way #415
Maitland, FL 32751
407.339.4217
www.xulonpress.com

© 2019 by Rosibel N. Hernandez

All rights reserved solely by the author. The author guarantees all contents are original and do not infringe upon the legal rights of any other person or work. No part of this book may be reproduced in any form without the permission of the author. The views expressed in this book are not necessarily those of the publisher.

Scripture quotations taken from the Holy Bible, New International Version (NIV). Copyright © 1973, 1978, 1984, 2011 by Zondervan. Used by permission. All rights reserved.

Printed in the United States of America.

ISBN-13: 978-1-54565-725-6

Dedication

This book is dedicated to my beloved parents. Without them, I would not be the woman I am today. They are God's precious gifts to me. My dad taught me what humility looks like. My mom has been my rock. Thank you, Mom and Dad, for your love and support throughout my lifetime.

To my brothers, Jorge and Wilson, they are my sun and my moon. Though I am the oldest of three siblings, they have taught me what love looks like beyond myself. They have demonstrated unconditional love through actions and have been there for me when I needed them most. I am forever grateful and blessed to be their sister.

Contents

Foreword by Pastor Jose R. Arce. xi

Introduction xv

Chapter One: The Ultimate Betrayal by a Man 1
Chapter Two: Forgiveness and Healing Begins 12
Chapter Three: An Unexpected Surprise –
   All in the Family 16
Chapter Four: Restoring the Years that Were Lost . . . 20
Chapter Five: A Mother's Heart and a Wife's
   Forgiveness 24
Chapter Six: A Commandment to Honor
   Thy Father. 30
Chapter Seven: Acts of Love. 34
Chapter Eight: The Man, The Husband,
   The Father 40
Chapter Nine: Forgiveness is a Must
   for Marriage. 45
Chapter Ten: The Ultimate Family Betrayal. 50
Chapter Eleven: The Kiss, The Traitor, The Savior 54
Chapter Twelve: He Makes All Things New. 59

Chapter Thirteen: Seven Steps to a
   Healed Heart 63
Chapter Fourteen: Scriptures of Forgiveness 67

Epilogue by Jorge L. Hernandez **69**

Foreword By:
Pastor Jose R. Arce

My impression when I read this book was that it may be short, yet it is impactful because of the complex topic it describes. In my opinion, few people have the courage to write about such intimate family issues. It gets even worse when it deals with a betrayal committed by one of your parents. Infidelity is a shameful issue that very few people choose to talk about.

I have personally known the author since her early childhood years. I know her testimony, her fidelity, and her service to the Lord. I also know her well-respected parents...what can I say? I know the whole family!

The author comes from hardworking parents who gave their children the best education they could afford. The kind of education they were not able to have for themselves. The author is a professional in every sense of the word.

After reading this book, I have come to the conclusion that it was never Rosa's intention to hurt her loved ones by telling her story. These episodes and situations were lived by the family and faced together. Occasionally, in our roles as parents, we make mistakes without any regards to the consequences it may bring to our family.

As she became aware of her father's infidelity, she began keeping it in her heart. By doing this, she created an atmosphere of pain, resentment, lack of confidence, and trust issues, which were destroying the image she had of her father. All of this caused a separation between Rosa and her father. She felt betrayed.

The story told here is not an effort to sympathize with those who are currently going through a similar ordeal. Neither is it trying to ally itself with those that have gone through a similar situation, but rather, to help us go deep into our hearts and find the starting point to find a solution to the betrayal.

In this book, Rosa speaks openly about her feelings as she discovered the infidelity of the person she admired the most: her role model, her hero, her father. From her perspective, he had stained

Foreword By: Pastor Jose R. Arce

the family honor. This feeling made Rosa close her heart, making both forgiveness and reconciliation completely unobtainable. This situation made Rosa label all men the same. Why treat them differently? They all deserved to be despised. She was deeply hurt and this made her unavailable for any serious romantic relationships. This took a toll on her, and she became emotionally and spiritually affected.

We can inflict so much pain upon our love ones when we act selfishly, especially, when we don't take into account the precious little souls, our children.

While Rosa meditated on the situation her family was going through, God started working on her heart. She learned to forgive. She realized she had to forgive her father the same way God had forgiven her. As soon as she opened her heart to forgive her father, he became the ray of light she had envisioned. This light started shining upon the whole family and changed them all for the good. Rosa understood forgiveness by practicing it. This brought a kind of healing no counselor could ever offer.

Forgiveness brings healing. It brings the prodigal son back home. It rebuilds broken relationships.

Betrayal by a Father and the Power of Forgiveness

It brings new beginnings. By forgiving, we are free to love unconditionally.

Today this young warrior, after having forgiven her father, is rejoicing in her peace. Furthermore, she has become her Heavenly Father's beloved child, as well as the beloved child of her father on earth. Nowadays, this father and daughter are a living testimony of what God can do when we listen to Him and practice what He has commanded us to do.

Who knows? Perhaps you, like Rosa, have had a similar experience and have not been able to forgive those who have betrayed you. Perhaps you have been betrayed by your father, your mother, your siblings, perhaps by a close friend. My advice to you is that you should fill yourself with strength from above and commit yourself to forgiveness. You will start noticing changes you never imagined in your life.

I admire Rosa, and I applaud her for such a valuable contribution to society in the form of this book.

Introduction

Before you begin to read my personal testimony, I want to clarify a few things. In essence, the term *Betrayal* according to Merriam-Webster dictionary is, **a violation of a person's trust or confidence.** The book title may be a bit strong, as my story is not meant to harm or discredit my father, nor men in general, but rather it is a journey of the power of true forgiveness and healing. Many people who have had to face situations where forgiveness was involved find themselves saying, **"I forgive you,"** or **"I accept your apology,"** but years down the road they seem to still remember the incident, which has morphed into anger and/or bitterness. True forgiveness holds no records, no grudges, no shame, and no guilt; mastering forgiveness can take a lifetime, but is definitely possible.

As many women and men alike have experienced infidelity in a marriage and/or father-daughter or son-mother relationship, the sense of betrayal is strongly felt. An emotional roller coaster sets in, causing people to entangle themselves in damaging or dysfunctional relationships. I can freely speak on this topic of dysfunctional relationships, because I unconsciously ruined relationships with men in my teens, twenties, and thirties, simply because I never got to the root of my own personal issues. It's not all daddy issues, but there are many factors that contributed to my messed-up relationships that were tied to my relationship with my father. Unfortunately, I learned a little later in life (thirties/forties) how to deal with my root issues that caused immense hurt for myself and the men who were in my life. The good news is that it's never too late to discover yourself and get the help you need to work on your issues.

The sole purpose of this book is to share my experience as a daughter, a sister, and a friend who understands hurt, hatred, anger, betrayal, and the true power of forgiveness. I also share how I overcame the deep-rooted issues, which allowed me to transition from a victim to a victor, from feeling angry to embracing freedom and joy. Come with me as I share this journey. I pray that as you read, you will be able to relate and understand there is a process to everything in life. Once the process is complete, there is freedom beyond imagination, which is the best feeling in the world.

I want to assure you, the chains of unforgiveness can be broken, but it will not happen overnight. You must be patient with the process and yourself. I have included steps to forgiveness and healing, which can be used to guide you through this process. My prayer is that you are set free and begin to enjoy life to the fullest!

Chapter One

The Ultimate Betrayal by a Man

Colossians 3:21
__21__ Fathers, do not embitter your children, or they will become discouraged.

Every child desires and deserves a loving home with parents who are their first role models, who can teach them to have healthy relationships through the example of a fruitful and happy marriage. Though this scenario is ideal, it's not always the case, such as was mine. When I was three years old, my parents and I left El Salvador and migrated to the USA. My brother, Jorge, who was only forty days old, was left behind with my grandmother until he was two years old, when my mom returned to get him. My brother and I were raised in one of the toughest inner-city neighborhoods of Washington, D.C., where many of my classmates never made it to high school, to college, or past their twenties. When I was growing up, my parents were hard-working people. They made sure to provide for my brother and I, but I was forced to fend for myself and my brother, protecting him from bullies, strangers, drug dealers, and any other harm in our neighborhood.

Our early childhood years were marked by lack of material goods, although we didn't know it. We did not have babysitters, we had cousins who were close in age and lived two blocks away, we all took care of each other. During these formative years, when kids depended on adults to care for them physically, I was the one who made sure my brother was safe, which developed my control issues at an early age. (I learned this during my counseling sessions, which I discuss later.)

My parents strived to live the American Dream for their children. They did not speak English well and had jobs that paid minimum wage, which is one of the reasons my dad was so adamant about my brother and me graduating from college. Thankfully, we both did. Although my parents provided the physical necessities, the only emotional support we had came from my mother's nurturing care. My father was emotionally and physically absent while working two jobs to make ends meet. My parents' tenacity and strong work ethic paid off, as the desired American Dream came true when they were business owners of the first barbershop.

I was eleven years old when we moved out of the rough neighborhood and transitioned to the suburbs of Montgomery County, Maryland. Talk about a huge adjustment for us all! I had completed the fifth grade when we left Washington, D.C., and now we were living in an area that was diverse, the education was better, and we actually had school buses to take us to and from school! We went from a one bedroom apartment to a duplex townhouse in a neighborhood where it was peaceful. There were no corner stores nearby where the drug dealers hung out, nor the sounds of gunshots. Major changes took place and we had to adapt quickly.

Through all these transitions, my parents continued to work hard, and once again, my dad was emotionally absent. He would show up whenever I caused havoc, as I was a bit of a rebel in my pre-teen and teen years. He took it upon himself to correct me when I was out of line, and I am thankful he did. Trust me, I was a handful during those years.

I need you to understand something very critical: a little girl or boy needs their father's affirmation in all areas of life. He is the first man he/she will meet in life and look up to as an example. The fathers' influence and role in their children's lives will prevail in many of their life decisions, including instilling an understanding of how a man should treat and respect a woman. The man, the husband, the father, the leader of the home, has more of an impact, whether positive or negative, than the mother. You may not agree with me, but it's true. The enemy has worked hard to strip men of their authoritative role in the home and in society. God is a God of order. HE made man the head of the home.

When Adam and Eve sinned, who did God question? It was Adam who had to account for their actions **(Genesis 3:1-10)**, so don't let anyone deceive you into thinking otherwise. God placed them in that order for a reason, and He has not wavered from this divine order since the beginning of time.

As the years passed, it was no secret that my father had infidelity issues that caused havoc in my parents' marriage. As I grew into my twenties, it inevitably had a greater impact on me. I never knew of the many affairs my dad had, because my parents kept grown-up issues out of sight.

My dad never physically abused my mother, but the emotional abuse with each affair chipped away her trust in him each time. I never saw public display of affection between them. Though I never heard them curse each other out or call each other names either, I am sure things were said behind closed doors. I was never one to meddle in my parents' marriage and never really thought about how happy they were, I just lived life in my own bubble.

In my late teens and early twenties, I started dating guys. I never had a serious official boyfriend, by the way. It was usually over before I knew it. I believe the longest "relationship" was a little over two months. I didn't respect them or care much about how I treated these guys, who were not bad. However, the condition of my heart was not good. It was full of distrust and just plain hard. I didn't realize how harsh my words were or how they made those guys feel when my actions were completely insensitive.

I was selfish and careless with my words. I had a strong, ruthless character. I was loyal to my friends, but when it came to boyfriend relationships, I was a mess! I am sure I scarred a few of these men for life. I am not kidding.

In 2000, I was 24 years old and attending college, totally focused on completing my undergraduate studies, attempting to figure out what career path I wanted, while also being involved in the family business - I had my plate full! Then all of a sudden, hell broke loose. A year prior to this, I was unaware of the drama unfolding. As I stated earlier, my parents were good at hiding things from my brother and me, but the following events came out in full effect.

In the spring of 1999, my dad traveled to El Salvador for a so-called business trip that quickly turned into an unexpected affair with a young lady who was younger than me! Things started to get interesting when my dad informed my mom that he would need more time to conduct business matters and could not come home. She became alert. A woman's intuition is almost never wrong. My mom decided to take a surprise trip to El Salvador, and lo and behold, the truth was staring her in the face. The hurtful thing was that everyone in the village, including family members, knew what was going on but did not say anything.

One of the first things my mother did was ask for a divorce. This was the straw that broke the camel's back, as the saying goes. Her patience and tolerance had come to an end. She felt humiliated, as the entire village knew what was going on. She was angry, hurt, and felt betrayed! This was the *first* time divorce was ever considered, the first

The Ultimate Betrayal By A Man

time she initiated and mentioned it. After twenty-five years of marriage, she was done! I had *no* clue what happened, because my dad begged my mom not to tell us, the kids. He knew this would damage his image even more in our eyes. She honored that request and did not tell us.

Of all my dad's affairs, this was the most damaging. Could it be because the woman was so much younger that she could have been his daughter (she was younger than me) or because my mom reached her breaking point? A woman comes to a breaking point in life. Whether in relationships, careers, or something else, there's a point of no return.

My dad begged her for forgiveness as my mother proceeded with initiating the divorce. I truly do not know how my mother mustered the strength not to tell my brother and me. We heard about it from other people. After much thought, counsel, and prayer, my mother decided not to proceed with the divorce. Part of her rationale was that you build a life with your spouse that includes a family, a home, several businesses, and properties. In other words, she worked hard and was not going to give it all up for another woman to enjoy the fruits of her hard labor. She refused to let that happen. She thought about my brother and me, as well. She wanted to keep the family together, in spite of the situation.

After things cooled off, my parents still loved each other, and my dad was my mother's first everything. They married very young, when she was seventeen years old and he was twenty-one years old. Their love story is powerful, in and of itself.

My maternal grandmother did not want my mom marrying my father because he didn't come from a prominent or wealthy family, so she plotted to get my dad arrested for "taking" my mom away, as she was under age. So my dad was immediately arrested and taken to jail. My mother was not going to let the love of her life suffer this injustice, so she decided to go to jail too. The whole village rose up and demanded they be released and let them marry. They were in custody for seventy-two hours. So in 1972, my grandmother backed off and allowed them to marry. Out of all my mother's eight siblings, her marriage has lasted the longest and strongest. There is no denying this crazy love story success.

In saying this, perhaps I will never understand my mother's reasoning for not moving forward with a divorce. Maybe their love story had something to do with it. Now my parents are in their senior years, and they rely more on each other than ever before.

When I found out about the affair, you can only imagine what I was going through emotionally. I had so much anger and bitterness in my heart toward my dad. So much so, these emotions manifested as trust issues toward men, even more than before.

How can I trust any man? How can I believe what other men say is true, when the only man I have loved and known from birth betrayed my mother, my brother, and me? How can he do this to our family? Hatred, resentment, and an inability to forgive became deep-rooted all at once in my heart.

By this time, I was close to twenty-five or so years old. My hope in men was shattered and any decent guy who crossed my path got a piece of my wrath. For months after I found out, anger, deep-rooted hurt, and (should I say it?) hatred toward my dad flared within me like never before. My love for him went out the window. The little respect I had for him was gone, and he knew it. I didn't curse my dad out. I never insulted him to his face or behind his back; I just had deep-rooted wounds from a father who betrayed us. I was devastated, to say the least.

At this stage in life, I was old enough to understand the importance of a father's faithfulness – or lack thereof. To see my mother in pain crushed my soul and took my spirit hostage! I begged my mother to divorce him. I begged her in private and in front of him. I had no reservations about expressing my feelings, which made my dad angry at me for voicing my request. He even threatened to whoop me for making the suggestion aloud. Shouting matches took place between my dad and me in a home that had no peace, but was rather a tense and unpleasant house. No longer a home, but just a plain house. There is a huge difference between a house and a home. I often imagined what life would be like without my dad. My brother and I discussed it and agreed that should a divorce occur, we both would live with Mom.

After my dad saw the immense damage his actions caused our family, he repented before God and asked the Lord to forgive him and to give him the strength to never cheat again. This took a lot of humility and a contrite heart for him to do this. This final affair was not kept behind closed doors. He and mom hashed it out in public. This was now a family affair, and a shattered home was the outcome. His wife was hurt and angry; the deceit was out in the open, and everyone knew about it. Most hurtful was that his kids' love for him was damaged. There was nowhere to turn to but to God.

Chapter Two

Forgiveness and Healing Begins

Psalm 147:3
***3** He heals the brokenhearted and*
binds up their wounds.

So how do I handle this deep-rooted pain caused by a father? How do I trust men again? How was I going to get over this tragic event – when, I was the last to know among family and friends. This was going to take serious time.

It was the spring of 2000 when I attended a women's retreat with my mom, is where things started to shift. During the final evening of the retreat, each woman received a personal card from a loved one. To my surprise, my dad had handwritten cards for both my mom and me. I was at one end of the huge room, and my mom was on the other end. As I read the card, tears came rolling down my face like a flood of water. It was so powerful. His words impacted me, asking me to forgive him for the affair and, most importantly, for the pain he caused our family. The entire card was filled with his heartfelt words, a side of my father I never knew existed. It was impactful and electrifying, and it was the start of what needed to be a key foundation to healing: true forgiveness.

My mom saw me crying uncontrollably from afar, she came over after I read the card, and asked me what my dad had written. I briefly told her. I didn't want to go into much detail because it was personal, something sacred between a father and a daughter. At that moment, the healing process started. It was not an easy road, but I was open to forgiving him and wanted to do it at my own pace, with the Lord's help. Never rush forgiveness, because you need time to digest and grieve, time to reflect, and time to understand why forgiveness is important.

True forgiveness requires not bringing up the past. It requires courage to start all over with that person who hurt you. It requires boldness, because people won't understand your motives and you are not obligated to explain. I thought my mom was insane for not proceeding with a divorce, but who was I to question her decision?

Three years later, complete healing took place. I had forgiven my dad, our home was restored, and I started a new journey after graduate school in 2005. My career was taking a new turn. It was exciting, it was unknown territory, and it was promising. I started a career that required living overseas, and my dad was an intricate part of my *new* journey. He helped me settle in to my new home overseas for the next few years, and when it was time for him to leave, my mom told me he cried at least three times on the plane. She was taken aback at how emotional he had become. In his eyes, he was leaving his little girl in a foreign land, with no one to look after her, unfamiliar with the language and culture. Nonetheless, deep inside he knew I was a survivor/warrior, and this was part of the journey.

During the years I was living overseas, I met new people and had a few God-ordained connections that helped shape my strong character at the time. It was a time of pruning my heart's condition. I had forgiveness in my heart, but I still had trust issues with men and it was evident by the way I continued treating them. I wasn't as mean, but I was tough in my dealings and handling them, especially toward a special man whom I met eight months before it was time to leave.

He too had a strong character, but I was the biggest challenge he had ever encountered, as he likes to put it. We both hurt each other and inflicted emotional pain as vengeance. Looking back now, we both realize how childish and immature we both were. Ahh – but you see, he was placed in my life as a self-check that I still needed healing and pruning, and the process continued. God will send people into your life. Though they may not be the "one," they are used for a reason, for a season, just to help mold your character and help you grow into a loving and patient person. If they are not for you, don't see it as rejection, but rather see them as someone who came to teach you life lessons.

During these eight months with that special man, we went through heartaches, good times, frustrating times, and pure enjoyment of a solid friendship that stood the test of trials and sincere forgiveness. We both knew we were good people, and we had learned a lot from each other, more than words can express. Appreciate good people, cherish the relationships, and be open to learning – no regrets.

Chapter Three

An Unexpected Surprise – All in the Family

Romans 8:28
__28__ And we know that in all things God works for the good of those who love him, who have been called according to his purpose.

Sin has unwanted consequences that must be dealt with without fear and without doubt. Even King David, who was a man after God's own heart, had to face consequences all the days of his life because of his affair with Bathsheba. You can find details to this story in **2 Samuel chapter 11**. What makes us think we can escape facing the consequences when we sin? This is something to think about, living in a world that doesn't focus much on the consequences from our careless actions.

The next series of events were unseen and inevitable. They forced us to come together as a strong family unit, and with much prayer we were able to embrace change. It took a huge adjustment and it wasn't a smooth transition, but God's unconditional love helped us along the way.

From the final affair in El Salvador in 1999, my dad unknowingly created a son. Our family did not know this until mid-2007, seven to eight years after the affair occurred. People in the village noticed a huge resemblance of my dad in the child, and they advised him to take a paternity test. I was on a trip in the mainland of where I was living overseas when I received the call from my dad. He told me about the situation and that he wanted to take a paternity test, but my mom threatened him with a divorce – yet another painful experience for my dear mother.

At this stage in my relationship with my dad, I was in a good place, and I was in full support of a paternity test. It was only fair for the child, who was not at fault for the sinful nature in which he was conceived. I had a woman-to-woman talk with my mom, calming her emotions and assuring her that we were all in this together as a family; she was not alone in this process.

Later that fall in 2007, my parents and I took a trip to El Salvador. My dad and I decided to go for a ride nearby. Purposely without my mother's consent, we went to visit my half-brother, who was only seven years old at the time. When I saw him, I fell in love! He was all dressed up, since we gave his mother and relatives a heads up that we were going to visit him. He was a bit shy but quickly warmed up to us both. My dad was taken by surprise at how much he looked like me with his chubby cheeks. He was adorable and full of energy. It wasn't long before my mom found out what happened. She was angry at both my dad and me. After two paternity tests (yes, we wanted to be sure), he was my dad's son.

Seeing this seven-year-old, who was full of energy, physically resembled me a lot, and embodied a few of my character traits, there was no denying this little human was my flesh and blood. I never once faulted him for this situation. As I invested more time with him, he won my heart and my love. Due to our huge age difference, I saw him as a son.

I want to pause here for a moment, as I need you to understand. When children are involved in situations like this, they are *not* to blame! On the contrary, they need to be embraced even more because society will try to label them as the "other child," as if they were an accident, so the children start to feel the impact of the cruel words and negative perception. In one or two incidents, people had referenced him in a negative way when introducing my brother Jorge and me to a group of people, and then nonchalantly referring to Wilson as the "other child." I got angry and took it upon myself to reinforce that Wilson was our brother – period!

Please do not put children in that position. It will impact them to think they are not part of the family, when in fact they are. They have your blood, your traits, and your demeanor. Do not dismiss them or refer to them as mistakes. Be mindful not to do this. Children are like sponges and absorb more than we can imagine.

Chapter Four

Restoring the Years that were Lost

Joel 2:25-26
__25__ I will repay you for the years the
locusts have eaten—
the great locust and the young locust,
the other locusts and the locust swarm—
my great army that I sent among you.
__26__ You will have plenty to eat, until you are full,
and you will praise the name of
*the L*ORD *your God,*
who has worked wonders for you;
never again will my people be shamed.

So, months later in 2008, it was time to go back overseas. My dad was my travel buddy again. It was a brutal winter when my dad and I arrived in the country, dark, gloomy, and cold. He helped me settle in, but little did he know the challenges we were going to face during his three-month stay. I got severely sick for a week, and my dad took good care of me.

While I was sick, my dad received news that his mother was dying in El Salvador. All six of his siblings were by her side, and my grandmother wanted my dad present. Faced with a difficult decision, whether to leave me sick in a depressing situation and go see his dying mother one last time, he decided to stay with me. That very moment in his decision to stay was a dramatic turning point in our relationship. There are moments in life that mark the trajectory of your path, and this was one of them.

I did not want my father to feel guilty for not being able to see his mother, so I prayed fervently that she would hang on until my dad was able to make it to El Salvador. God granted my prayer, my dad was able to see and hold his mother one last time, as my grandmother hung on to life long enough to see her son's face again before she took her last breath of life.

During this time before my dad departed for El Salvador, our relationship grew closer as we spent quality time together. We spent weekends shopping, cooking together, attending social events, traveling throughout the region, and even taking a get-away trip to Italy. It was an experience of a lifetime alongside my father, who was now one of my best friends. We discovered each other's character, personalities, likes and dislikes, and just like that, we were creating a bond that was never there before.

I started to appreciate and respect my dad for the man he was, which was a new experience for me. He took good care of me during my sick days, waited at the metro stop for me so he could walk me home, cooked dinner for me, and even ironed my clothes. As I was at work all day, my dad took it upon himself to shower me with these acts of love. I didn't realize at the time, because of my immaturity and lack of experience, this was his *love language*. Not only for me, but our family.

True forgiveness was setting in, and I can attest, it is an amazing experience – it is liberating, empowering, and it breaks chains! The power of forgiveness restores years of hate, grudges, remorse, and bitterness. No longer was I being robbed of a genuine, loving relationship with my father. God was restoring and rebuilding what the enemy tried to destroy. When you don't forgive, you are giving the enemy power!

In the spring of 2011, our lives forever changed. My little brother was coming to live with us in the USA. He was only eleven years old when he decided to leave everything he ever knew, including his mom, and go to the unfamiliar country and to an unknown family. His world and our world changed dramatically. We had this little person who didn't know much about life in our home.

We taught him what a family looked like and showed him unconditional love, not to mention instilling godly principles for everyday living. We treated and loved him as if we were biological siblings and he had been a part of our lives all along. My mom quickly gained his trust and love. It was a mutual feeling between them. This life-changing event was a family affair. We had to make this work. God causes *all* things to work together for the good.

Chapter Five

A Mother's Heart and a Wife's Forgiveness

Proverbs 31:25-31
25 *She is clothed with strength and dignity;*
she can laugh at the days to come.
26 *She speaks with wisdom,*
and faithful instruction is on her tongue.
27 *She watches over the affairs of her household*
and does not eat the bread of idleness.
28 *Her children arise and call her blessed;*
her husband also, and he praises her:
29 *"Many women do noble things,*
but you surpass them all."
30 *Charm is deceptive, and beauty is fleeting;*
*but a woman who fears the L*ORD *is to be praised.*
31 *Honor her for all that her hands have done,*
and let her works bring her praise
at the city gate.

I want to take a moment and share the characteristics of my mother during this entire journey. She exemplifies the Proverbs 31 woman, specifically verses 25 to 31, and here is why. While I was going through my own emotions, I never pondered or took into consideration my mother's feelings and her decision to stay in the marriage. The craziest decision that blows people's minds was taking in the child who was not her own, as if he were her own son. I asked her, "What made you take him in?" and she quickly replied, "Seeing this child, who wasn't even ten years old, suffering and practically raising himself, touched my heart profoundly."

She displayed the true heart of a loving mother. The love between my little brother and mother is unexplainable. It's a special bond. She once told him, "I didn't give birth to you, but you're still my child." My mother's love for him is unwavering. She prays and covers him, she has defended him when needed, and much more.

I once asked my little brother in a casual conversation, "Who prays the most for you in this house?" He gently and quickly replied, "Mrs. Corina (my mom)." He knows he is wanted, loved, and adored – he was not a mistake, and he has purpose and a calling on his life, in spite of life's situations.

Let us put ourselves in my brother's shoes: you were not conceived in love but rather lust. At only eleven years old, you came to the USA to an unknown family and didn't know how they would receive or treat you. You had no idea the life you were embracing, as you were used to living in the streets without a stable family structure or somewhere to call home, because your mother didn't take good care of you. In 2018, I asked my brother to pray as we were asking the Lord for some things. Two minutes into his prayer, he thanked God for his family!

Up until that moment, he didn't feel part of the family, though he was already living with us for seven years. He felt as if he were the "other child." We love him so much, and we always made sure he was included in all things as a family. There is no half-brother; there is only blood-brother for life. He doesn't have to worry about abandonment or lack of love. We cherish and love him as he is.

Now, let's take a look at Hagar and Ishmael. Not exactly the ideal situation. However, that didn't stop the Lord from blessing Ishmael **(Genesis 17:20)**. Just because things didn't pan out how you expected them to, that doesn't mean God won't bless it or make the best out of the situation. My mother did what she felt led to do in her heart.

She didn't let society and their opinions change her mind or her decision or love for my brother. As she sees it, she gained a son, as we gained a brother whom we love very much.

My mother's decision to stay in the marriage kicked the enemy in the tail. She refused to break her family apart and *fought* hard for it. Of course, the Bible does justify divorce due to infidelity, but there is also a choice to stay. My mom was always a fighter, and resilience runs in her DNA. She doesn't give up easily and maintains herself grounded in her walk with the Lord. She's a prayer warrior and stays true to who she is, no matter what is happening around her. She's solid, and because of her faithfulness to God, she now has a daughter (me) who displays these same attributes.

Through her decision to stay in the marriage, my mom broke generational curses of divorce in her family. She is the only one who has stayed married to the same man for over 45 years. Women, please understand, making this decision does *not* make you a weak person; it makes you a stronger and wiser person! It takes courage, boldness, and humility to stand on the decision to stay in a marriage that merits a justifiable divorce.

Your choices and decisions in life have the power to make or break generational curses or blessings.

Are you willing to sacrifice for the generations to come? Think about this the next time you are faced with difficult decisions. My mom sought wise counsel and prayed a lot before making the decision to stay. Looking back, I am glad she did, as my parents approach their **50th** wedding anniversary.

Their marriage may not have been the most ideal, but there was respect and genuine love in spite of the trials. My mom's gentle yet strong spirit is admirable. After all she has been through, she has wholeheartedly forgiven my dad, holding no grudges, nor bringing up the past. She is a fierce leader in her own right. She has been criticized for staying, but at the end of the day, you have to live with your decisions, not other people's opinions. She is at peace with her decision, and that's all that matters. Her children adore her, she is praised for the woman that she is, she speaks with wisdom, and her husband knows she is a diamond of a wife. She is a Proverbs 31 woman. My mother is a warrior, and I have high admiration for her achievements as a wife, mother, business woman, friend, sister, and daughter of the King of Kings.

If you are faced with the decision to divorce, I urge you to pray and seek wise counsel beforehand. God is a restorer of all things. Rest assure, He is no respecter of persons; He can do it for you too. Whatever you are going through, remember, this too shall pass, and you will come out on the other side like refined gold, strong and unbreakable. Please do not concern yourself with society's opinions. They don't matter. What truly matters is what you feel is best for your marriage, for your children, and most importantly, what God reveals in your heart and what needs to be done. ***Do not give up. Fight for your marriage!***

Chapter Six

A Commandment to Honor Thy Father

Exodus 20:12
__12__ Honor your father and your mother, so that you may live long in the land the L<small>ORD</small> your God is giving you.

I remember it clear as day when my dad and I got into a heated argument in 2014 over an issue regarding my little brother. Voices were loud, and anger ran wild within me. I walked away and went straight to my room for the evening. The entire night, I could not sleep; I had a heaviness in my spirit, and the Lord plugged away at my heart to ask my dad for forgiveness for the tone I used. Though I was correct regarding what we argued about, my delivery and tone were out of order!

The next day, I was eager to ask for forgiveness, but my pride was still a problem. My dad had left early to take my brother to school, and I thought, "Good, I don't have to face him now; I can do it later." Well, that didn't go as I hoped. As soon as I was opening the door to leave to go to work, my dad was coming in. It took a lot for me to apologize, but I did it.

My dad bowed his head and said, "Don't worry about it."

I am sure he wasn't expecting a quick apology from his stubborn daughter, who thought she was right. I felt relieved, and my dad's humbleness in accepting my apology melted my heart and kicked my pride to the side!

I share this story because our tone and how we deliver a message can impact our relationships. This situation in particular was a matter of respecting and honoring my father. I was not honoring him with my tone. I was rude and out of my place as his daughter. I was quickly rebuked and was corrected by my Heavenly Father. The Bible gives us clear instructions and warnings about life circumstances, one of which is commanding us to honor thy father and thy mother, in that order, whether we like it or not, so that we will have long and full lives.

Take a moment to digest this.

For some of you, this may be almost impossible. You may not have a relationship of any kind with your father, or perhaps your dad passed away and you didn't have the opportunity to forgive. I have good news: *today*, you can ask the Lord to change you and give you strength to first forgive yourself, and second, to forgive your earthly father.

When we put ourselves in our fathers' shoes, let's look at how they were reared. My dad grew up seeing his dad have two women his whole life, his mother and the mistress who lived in the neighborhood. This would traumatize or instill those warped "family values" in a child who saw and lived it while trying to figure life out. That was my dad's model of a family structure, and it was normal. When I saw things from that perspective, I became understanding and compassionate with my dad. The same with my mom, who didn't have a family structure either. There was no real father figure in the home, and she and her siblings pretty much raised themselves with no real parental support; although my grandmother was around, she didn't know how to properly raise children. Yet somehow, my parents made it work and stuck together.

My dad shared with me in 2018 that despite his affairs, leaving us (my mom and his children) was never an option. He had women who tried to persuade him to leave my mom, and he would end the affair quickly, because that was not going to happen. What I want to convey is: examine how your father was reared, so you can have a concept of why he is the way he is. This is not to grant him an excuse for doing wrong, because I believe people can change despite their upbringing, but rather to give you a sense of understanding of where it all stems from.

Today, my family is stronger, closer, and most importantly, we are a testament to what forgiveness looks like. My dad is a better father, a better husband, and most importantly, an unwavering servant of the Lord. He is my world, my heart, and I can't see my life without him. I enjoy giving him hugs and kisses, and most importantly, I love serving my dad through actions.

Chapter Seven

Acts of Love

1 Peter 4:8
*__8__ Above all, love each other deeply,
because love covers over a multitude of sins.*

Growing up with Dad was challenging, as he never spoke words of love, nor was he affectionate toward his loved ones. However, looking back, I now realize his love language has always been and will continue to be through acts. When he decides to talk, those words have major impact. Here are a few examples of his acts of love.

After I graduated from high school in 1994, I decided to take a class in college just to see if college was for me. Since I already had my barber's license and I was already working in the family business, I didn't see a reason why I should pursue a college degree. My first college course was an

English class, and I failed miserably! I admit, I didn't put effort into it, since I thought the class was going to be a breeze. When the final grade came in, I was devastated – I got a D. Not a C as in "good," but D as in "failed"!

I had the letter with the result in hand as I sat on my bed, crying and thinking, "I am dumb; this is not for me." So my father, in all his wisdom and gentleness, came into my room while I was crying, sat next to me, and said, "You cannot give up so quickly."

The following words had a huge impact on me. They gave me the courage to go back to college and not give up.

He said, "A good education is something no one can ever take away from you - ever!"

Those words resonated within me for decades. Those words coming from a father who did not finish elementary school because he had to work and survive. He gave me those heartfelt words to sooth my pain and rid my doubts. Those tender, wise words were a turning point for me and my future.

I wiped my tears after he left my room and the very next day I enrolled in a few more classes, including the class I had failed. Needless to say, my parents attended both my undergraduate and graduate ceremonies with such honor and proud looks on their faces. These were priceless moments I have engraved in my heart and spirit. Those degrees were also the accomplishments of amazing parents, who supported and invested in my education, as well as my brother Jorge's.

Many parents live vicariously through their children's accomplishments, and this was one of those moments. Though my dad wanted my brother Jorge and me to choose a career in accounting, which neither of us picked, he didn't stop us from doing what we wanted to do. He was and continues to be supportive each step of the way.

Another example of my dad's act of love was the summer of 1999, Rap Fest in the Bronx, NY. The year before this event happened, I returned to the Lord. I had strayed away for a few years. In those few years, I had a taste of how life was like without the Lord, but the Holy Spirit kept pulling me to get my life straight and get back on track. Within one year, God took away friends who were not a part of my future. I didn't have the urge to go clubbing. I stopped smoking (I only smoked for a month or so). I dumped my boyfriend and told the Lord, "If I come back, I don't want a boyfriend, I want a husband." Well, God listened, and I never had a boyfriend since then; the worldly desires were no longer within me. It was nothing but God who shifted my life dramatically.

A year later, after rededicating my life to the Lord, I met new friends who were Christians and had the same interests as me, including a love for rap music. So we made plans to go to New York and attend Rap Fest in the Bronx. Christian artists were performing all day in a huge, outdoor block party. It was my first experience of its kind. My mom, who was concerned that my friends and I were planning to go, made my father go with us to make sure I was "safe." I had traveled to New York many times before this, but was now being chaperoned to the event with my new friends while my dad drove, all of us squeezed into my mom's Nissan Pathfinder. How embarrassing for me! My mom made it clear: I could not go unless my dad went. I had no choice, so we took a five-hour drive to the Bronx.

When we arrived, we were so happy and excited. The place was packed, blocks and blocks of artists and people, young people, having a great time! My dad, on the other hand, after a couple of non-stop live rap music performances, decided to explore the neighborhood and leave the "noise" to get some sanity. He left for hours. I had no clue what he did all that time, nor did I ask, as I was having a good time! He finally showed up and we left late, and he drove us back home. Through this act of love to protect and make sure I wasn't going to get in any kind of trouble, I can now say and realize: this was definitely an act of selfless love!

One final example was when I was a key youth leader in 2001 at my church. I hosted a talent show. The purpose of this event was to raise money for the youth, and there were many participants, judges, and sponsors. It was a *fun,* action-packed event. My dad, in support of the event and my efforts, decided to participate and use his singing abilities. He picked a "mariachi" song, not ideal for the youth, but he sang his little heart out with enthusiasm and passion. Though most of the youth didn't take it into account, the older generation were pleasantly entertained, as my father loves to sing and does it from the heart. I didn't appreciate that genre of music at the time. However, I now have it on my playlist, and I love it. I fell in love with the music and the songs my dad sings. After this event, my dad was given singing opportunities, either at the church or special occasions. He should have recorded an album by now, but he is content with his own home studio. He sings and records whenever he can; days off, Sundays after church – this man loves to sing!

I wanted to share these experiences because you must understand, every person is different. This includes how they express and show their love. I was naive and still carried deep-rooted pain, which didn't allow me to see the unconditional and sincere love that my father was demonstrating through actions. He didn't know any other way to say, "I love you," without displaying it through uncomfortable situations. They say actions speak louder than words. Well, now I can attest to this saying as I reflect and ponder on my father's love for me.

Please take the time to study your loved ones and find out how they show their love and concern for you. It's not enough to judge them for lacking in one area, but it's important to know how they express themselves without trying to change them. My family in general are not emotional, mushy human beings, but I am. I love smothering them with hugs and kisses as well as cooking a family meal to share. I love showering my parents with affection, as I know both of them were not brought up that way. They know it's my way of showing love, so they let me hug and kiss them – hugs heal, restore, and strengthen the soul.

Chapter Eight

The Man,
The Husband, The Father

2 Corinthians 5:17
17 *Therefore, if anyone is in Christ,*
the new creation has come: The old has gone,
the new is here!

Man sees the outward appearance, but God and only God sees the heart. Being men is hard enough, as they are called to be the protectors and providers for the family. Talk about pressure and stress. Besides being accountable for the outcome of the family, there is a lot at stake when you have such responsibilities on your shoulders. Society has stripped men of their self-worth. Men are also emotional beings, and women forget that. It's time to stop bashing men. If you have had a bad experience with a man, please do not let that deter you from giving another man a chance to demonstrate his love. Do not let one more man pay for another man's mistakes. Let's take a moment to praise the good men and see the good in them.

My journey with my dad has forced me to face the reality of putting myself in his shoes to process and genuinely forgive. For instance, my dad has had to make financial decisions, business deals, and other key decisions that could bless or burden the family. I can proudly say my dad has been an amazing provider to our family. Also, he always made sure we would move forward as a family, from success to success. There were some setbacks here and there, but we always moved forward.

I can tell you, without a shadow of a doubt, my father has evolved into a better man, a better father, and an amazing husband. My dad did things with my younger brother, Wilson, that he didn't do with Jorge and me. He actually read bedtime stories with Wilson. He took time to have quality talks with him too. He wanted to do things the right way and realized his presence trumped his presents. Nothing can substitute for a father's quality time with his children.

As a husband, my father never stood in the way of my mother's development as an adult woman or as a career woman. He always supported her efforts, from when she learned how to drive, to getting her driver's license, to getting her master's barber license, to opening her own business and allowing her to contribute to decisions that were pertinent to the family. My father never demanded that my mother stay home and cook. On the contrary, my dad is quite the cook and knows how to maintain a clean home. I don't know if his time in the military in El Salvador had anything to do with this training, but my dad can run a home without feeling like less than a man.

My dad has always encouraged my mother to excel and do better and was not afraid to let her shine. He knows the quality of wife and woman my mother is, and he has never left her side, in spite of his mistakes. Leaving her under any circumstances was never an option. Today, they enjoy each other, they take care of one another, and they have a genuine and solid marriage. This is a love that has evolved to be stronger than ever before.

Though my dad's relationship with my brother, Jorge, isn't what I would hope, it has become better. Restoration happens when all parties are willing to make a change. When Jorge could not move physically because he had a minor surgery in 2009, my dad made sure his son had food and was recovering well. He went grocery shopping for him and cared for him. With Wilson, he accompanied him to look for employment and made sure he was taken care of, and he gave him the love his biological mom didn't give him. My dad loves his sons and his daughter. His past experiences have taught him to be a better father.

Two major traits that I learned from my dear father are confidence and humility. He has never exhibited fear in any of his abilities or endeavors and has always maintained a calm confidence in his abilities. He is a man of many skills, from building furniture, to making clothes, to cutting hair, to doing anything and everything that would be productive and fruitful. He did it with assurance and meekness. I have never seen my father fall apart. Instead, I have witnessed his strengths, which are admirable. I learned this confidence from him, so it is innately in me. I have had many people mistake my confidence for cockiness. Arrogance is one thing, and confidence is another. Make sure not to confuse the two, because there is a huge difference.

My dad had a hard life, working from a young age doing jobs no one wanted to do, yet he never let those experiences define him as a man. He was mistreated for being a minority when he first arrived in the USA. He didn't speak the language, but made the efforts to learn it and have full conversations with people from all walks of life. My father earned the right to flaunt material things due to his successes. However, he chose to provide for his family and made sure his children didn't have to worry about school loans or where their next meal would come from. He spoiled us and made sure we would be well taken care of before he lavished anything on himself. My dad knows who he is, where he came from, and how far the Lord has brought him and blessed him. He does not take these things for granted.

My dad is not perfect, but his heart is pure and God knows him like the palm of His hand. I can't imagine my life without my dad. He brings me joy, has an adventurous spirit, and is open for change and confident in who he is, with humility. There is not an ounce of pride in him, but he is a pure soul who had quite a journey in life. My dad is a fighter. He had his weak moments, as well as moments of realization to help him change and be a better man, a better husband, and a better father. I am so proud to be his daughter. He is my world.

Chapter Nine

Forgiveness is a Must for Marriage

Mark 11:25
__25__ And when you stand praying, if you hold anything against anyone, forgive them, so that your Father in heaven may forgive you your sins.

This book isn't necessarily about marriage, but I wanted to cover this topic, as I believe preparation for marriage is vitally important and the subject of forgiveness is something we must master before walking down the aisle. You will find yourself needing to forgive your spouse over and over again, without holding grudges and/or bitterness. Through my experiences with my earthly father, I learned this through the years. Learning to forgive and forget quickly is key to a successful marriage. Although I am not yet married, my married friends can attest to this truth. If you are thinking about marriage, single people, talk to happy and healthy couples. I now want to share the following life experience, as God has been preparing me for enriching and fruitful relationships.

In my mid to late twenties, a desire for marriage started to develop, but I was far from ready to make a lifetime commitment. I wanted to complete graduate school, explore international travel, find a career that I would be passionate about, and achieve financial goals before settling down. Once I achieved these goals, I was in my early thirties, I *thought* I was ready for marriage. However, I needed to make sure I no longer had trust issues with men. Over the years, I learned if you want to have a healthy and happy marriage, trust is the foundation to build upon. Without it, a relationship may never last.

My trust issues with my dad spilled over to my non-existent relationships with men. I decided early on that no one would hurt me. And if things didn't go my way, then I would pick on a minor flaw and use excuses why the man would not work out. Furthermore, I was *super* mean to guys. There were a handful whom I treated horribly with my lack of compassion and sympathy. I was hard to break. I went as far as saying vile words, and I never apologized for anything, as I didn't see an issue in my actions. In my life, I fell in love maybe one or two times, and even with those guys, I was horrible! I was very guarded and put every ounce of energy into school, career aspirations, and completing goals that didn't involve relationships. After all, I could control those other things, but matters of the heart I could not control, so I was safe in staying guarded... can you relate to this?

In 2012, I was thirty-six years old and decided to seek counseling for a year to address my concerns that developed early in life. A friend referred me to a counselor, and to my surprise, she was a marriage counselor. A perfect match for me.

The counselor asked me during our first session, "Why are you here?"

I replied, "Because I want to prepare for marriage."

She was taken aback and said, "You are so wise in doing this before you marry – I wish more people were as proactive as you!" It was a great year!

Now in my forties, I not only have a healthy, loving relationship with my father, but also with men, although I am still working on my control issues. We are all still a work in progress. In the fall of 2015, God started to speak heavily to me on **1 Peter chapter 3,** and for the following two years, I started to understand the role of a wife, the role of a husband, and what a healthy marriage is supposed to look like. It's never too late to learn and recognize your flaws so you can make changes accordingly.

God brought married women who had strong marriages into my life, to show me the key traits of a wife through their own experiences/situations and to pray for me; these experiences could not be learned from my single friends. The Lord kept speaking to me about having a soft, gentle spirit, and I didn't know what that looked like. Throughout my entire life I was surrounded by strong women. My bloodline from my mother's side has strong-willed women, including my beloved mother. Therefore, I didn't know what submission looked like, or what a soft and gentle spirit entailed. How was I going to change at forty-plus years old? Let's just say God started the work in 2017 and continues to work on my character. I will stop with this topic here because I don't want to get into the weeds of preparing for a God-centered marriage. But the truth remains: build a strong relationship with your father if you want to have a strong marriage.

Not all fathers are perfect. There is only one – the Heavenly Father – who is perfect and who forgives. You have to forgive your earthly father, no matter what the situation may be. Ladies, how can you marry a man when you still haven't forgiven your father? Or men, how can you marry a woman when you haven't forgiven your mother? Forgiveness is not just for that person; it is for you.

Forgiveness is freedom, and it will bring true healing to your soul. Again, if you are single, you must try to have a respectful relationship with your father before marriage, because it could be a strong indication of how you will view your husband. The power of inner healing will open your eyes to view things differently, more powerfully, more purposefully, and will bring peace to your mind and soul.

Chapter Ten

The Ultimate Family Betrayal

Genesis 45:4
4 "I am your brother Joseph,
the one you sold into Egypt!

I want to take a moment and share a powerful example of betrayal and forgiveness. Let us take an in-depth look at the book of Genesis, which includes a very familiar passage many of us have read and heard many times, but few have studied and processed this series of events. The story takes place in chapters 37 through 46, which most people know as the ultimate family betrayal and the power of forgiveness. I want to focus on this because it is specific to family members, especially those closest to you. In this case, it was siblings. We have all heard of "sibling rivalry," but Joseph's brothers give it a whole new and crazy meaning.

The Ultimate Family Betrayal

Can you imagine being sold because of jealousy and hate from your own flesh and blood? I have two younger brothers, and I could never fathom doing such a cruel and atrocious thing!

Joseph was seventeen years old or so when he was sold and taken to an unfamiliar land, where the customs, culture and religion were very different. He had to quickly adapt to his new life and environment while dealing with the pain of family betrayal and the sadness of never seeing his family. Particularly his younger brother, Benjamin, who had nothing to do with the betrayal, and his aging father, whom he adored.

At that time, there were no "counselors" or anyone he could confide in or vent to. It was only him and God, going through the process of grieving, healing, and slow restoration. During his time in Egypt, Joseph was put into situations that tested his loyalty to God and his own principles. Joseph was well-respected among the elite, powerful Egyptians, including the untouchable Pharaoh. Joseph was a man of integrity. He never allowed his life circumstances to change who he was as a person, and he didn't hold on to grudges. He withstood the time of pressure and quickly gained wisdom and maturity through his array of experiences, but the fact remained, his very own flesh and blood sold him into slavery. I am sure the wounds were deep-rooted.

After Joseph rose to power, he was only thirty years old and immediately had a family of his own. He never imagined being able to see his family again. However, an extreme famine brought his brothers to Egypt, and interestingly enough, Joseph immediately recognized them. By contrast, his brothers had no clue who he was, as Joseph was royalty and very powerful. He was no longer the kid with the wild dreams, but rather his presence demanded respect and reverence.

Let's look closely to chapter 45, when Joseph revealed himself to his brothers. *He wept loudly* while embracing his brothers! It took boldness, courage, and humility for Joseph to make this move. He sent off his staff to have a private moment of revelation with his siblings, the people who sold him, who turned their backs on him, who denied him, and who kept the truth from their father. Joseph's tears were liberating. The deep hurt of betrayal he had buried all those years was finally being released.

Pause for a moment. Isn't it funny how years fly by after an unfortunate event? You think it's over and done with and you are "healed," when all of a sudden, it stares you in the face or something occurs that would promptly open that "closed" wound. The

The Ultimate Family Betrayal

wound was never closed to begin with. Instead, it was patched up nicely, but the deep-rooted wound remained. I can talk freely about this from personal experience. A man whom I thought I was supposed to be with did something that was totally unforgivable. As years went by, I forgave him, but the scars that it left did damage to other men whom I dealt with. For example, if I remotely thought they were disrespecting me by flirting with other women, that wound just opened up quickly. This remained a vicious cycle until I gave that hurt over to God, completely over to *Him,* for me to be healed and whole.

Every time I read the story of Joseph in the Bible, I cry. It moves me to the core. If you are having a hard time forgiving a family member, I implore you to read this story over and over again. Study and take time to digest it, because I can guarantee it will help you to forgive when you thought it wasn't possible. Like in Joseph's case, what the devil meant for evil, God turned for good! Trust God to give you strength and courage to forgive. Don't let the enemy rob you of joy and a fulfilled life. Joseph lived a full and blessed life, although he suffered a bit while building a strong foundation of forgiveness that led to complete family restoration and wholeness. Joy is on the other side of forgiveness.

Chapter Eleven

The Kiss, The Traitor, The Savior

Mark 14:44
44 Now the betrayer had arranged a signal with them: "The one I kiss is the man; arrest him and lead him away under guard.

Let me start by asking a question: Have you ever been betrayed by a friend who was closer than a brother? I have, and it's a different type of betrayal, a different wound, a different hurt. I would like to take a closer look at this famous, piercing, and life-changing story. Imagine breaking bread, having wisdom instilled, being mentored and nurtured by a good friend for whom you left the known to join on a journey. The man who did this witnessed miracles and was known as part of the most powerful group of men, the famous twelve disciples.

He witnessed his mentor calm the seas, raise the dead, heal the blind, and feed thousands of people. Such was the life of Judas, who lived day to day with Jesus, the son of God. Judas walked alongside Jesus every single day, while experiencing these miracles, yet felt compelled to betray Him for thirty pieces of silver. What would trigger you to do such a tragic betrayal against a beloved friend who was like a big brother?

Such betrayal ultimately led Judas to killing himself. I can't imagine the torture he went through, emotionally and mentally. Betraying the King of Kings, the Savior of the world, the friend who embraced him closer than His own family, who invited him on this glorious journey of spreading the gospel and sharing the good news. What possessed him to do such a thing? Could it have been greed, the need for attention or to be accepted by the Romans, who were a powerful kingdom at the time; jealousy, or envy that caused Judas to do this?

Perhaps you have been in a situation where a friend behaved in a treacherous manner, and you had no clue what you did that caused such behavior. You got hurt and carried the wound for quite some time without taking the time to reflect and heal properly. I want you to give yourself permission to grieve, forgive, and heal.

Now on the other hand, imagine Jesus, who was praying fervently, asking God to take this cup of suffering away **(Luke 22:42)**. Jesus knew the inhuman torture that was coming, when He was going to be the ultimate sacrifice for our sins. He endured such pain for us to the point that He was unrecognizable before they hung Him on a tree. This was no easy task, and Jesus rightfully asked the Father to take this cup away. But Jesus also acknowledged His earthly assignment, and so He chose to move forward and complete the God-given assignment.

Furthermore, Jesus knew one of the disciples was going to betray Him with a kiss, and He announced it while they broke bread one last time. Can you imagine – you are fully aware of the torture, agony, and pain you were going to go through, and then on top of all that, your very own disciple was going to lead your enemy to your hiding place of prayer? Jesus bore it *all*!

In spite of such pain and betrayal, I am certain Jesus would have forgiven Judas. However, Judas couldn't forgive himself. If you have ever been a Judas, I want you to know Jesus already forgave you. I would suggest you apologize to the person you hurt, and if they don't want to accept the apology, you at least can feel free, and hopefully you learned a valuable lesson to never do it again. Perhaps we will never know why Judas betrayed Jesus with a kiss, but the fact remains, friends betray friends at some point in life. Sometimes that betrayal is more hurtful than if a family member had done it. In true friendships, there is a special bond that is formed. We see examples of these powerful friendship bonds between Jonathan and David, Ruth and Naomi, Paul and Timothy – these bonds are unbreakable. They are unique and special. They are to be preserved and treated with respect. However, sometimes things don't go quite as we had hoped. We then have to follow the example of Jesus. There will be moments where you will need time alone to process, and I suggest you not rush this process. Take your time.

I implore you to study in-depth this story of Jesus and Judas. Most importantly, put yourself in Jesus' shoes. In 2014, I was in a situation where I did not have the option to back out. I was really upset and frustrated, when one day I was in my room and opened the Bible to the scripture of the prayer of Jesus asking God to take the cup away. It popped out like a sore thumb!

As I read it, I was immediately convicted and went to take a shower, where I poured my heart to the Lord (I cried *sooo* hard!), knowing Jesus went through something He had no desire to do, yet did it because of His love for us and obedience to the Father. He also knew His assignment and what was at stake if He didn't go through with it.

Exactly a year after I went through that particular situation, I came out like refined gold, a sparkling diamond, and stronger because I was obedient and completed the task at hand. What are you facing today that would have you conflicted, angry, hurt, or saddened? Spend time with the Savior, who hears you and knows every tear, and most importantly, He understands your situation. Trust Him through it all.

Chapter Twelve

He Makes All Things New

Isaiah 43:18-19
18 "Forget the former things;
do not dwell on the past.
19 See, I am doing a new thing!
Now it springs up; do you not perceive it?
I am making a way in the wilderness
and streams in the wasteland.

Life is not a fairy tale. Life has real problems, real consequences, and real solutions. My story is a fraction of what many have faced or will face at some point in their lives. We can't stop things from happening, but we must confront them when needed. You cannot hide from what has happened. You must deal with it head-on. It is during these tumultuous and trying times that our character is being stretched, tested, and pressed!

I implore you to take time to reflect on matters of the heart, events that have shattered your world, or perhaps you are at a crossroads where you don't know what to do and you have fallen into depression or complete solitude. It is okay to be in this position. Give yourself time to grieve and heal, but *do not* stay there! I can attest to the pain of depression, where you don't want to deal with people at any level. You want to sleep away the issues, cry until your eyes are puffy, and leave to never return, but God doesn't work that way. He wants us to confront the issues in the appropriate timing and with the right attitude.

In **Genesis 16:7-13,** Hagar ran away from home while pregnant because Sarah was giving her a hard time and made her feel unwanted. The angel of the Lord appeared to Hagar and told her to go back and face Sarah. The angel also had a name for the child, Ishmael, and promised the child a future, in spite of the situation! Ishmael, by the way, means "God hears," and indeed He heard Hagar's cries, agony, pain, and misery, and still made sure she and her child were provided for and protected. **God never fails**! Some things we will never comprehend, but God has *all* the solutions. *Trust Him.*

Let's take a look at someone else who fled and decades later was commanded to return. To whom

He Makes All Things New

am I referring? Moses. If you have not read it, you may be familiar with the story where Moses murdered an Egyptian, fled, and for years never saw Egypt. Yet those years were being used to prepare Moses for the tedious task ahead **(Exodus 4:18-29)**. Those years of preparation were used to form Moses' character and to build endurance, courage, and strength as he was being groomed to lead God's people to the Promised Land. You think it was easy to return to the land where you were wanted for murder? Or facing the most powerful ruler at the time and demanding he let the Israelites, God's chosen people, leave Egypt? This was no easy task, yet Moses mustered the faith and boldness to do it. When God instructs you to do something, He prepares and equips you to execute His divine plan, and nothing can stop it!

In this life, you too will be asked to confront your past or your pain so you can move forward to your promises. You will not be able to enjoy your promises without sacrifice and willingness to put pride to the side and forgive those who have wounded you. Do not rob your future by ignoring your hurts. You owe it to yourself and your generation to forgive and be free.

Thank you for allowing me to share my story and journey of forgiveness. My prayer is that it will help you and your future relationships, but most importantly, that you will establish at least a cordial relationship with the person who has hurt you beyond words. I pray you are set free and can start to enjoy life at a new level. True freedom begins when you forgive, even when you do not get an apology. Forgiveness brings healing and health. Did you know that an unforgiving heart makes you ill? Set yourself free and start enjoying life **NOW**.

Every day brings new challenges, but nothing is impossible to attain or achieve. Never conform to just living day by day with bitterness and remorse. You were born for greatness and deserve a fulfilling life filled with joy and true freedom. Once you come to a place of inner peace and a heart that has room for forgiveness, you are now living a new life. The best is yet to come! The promises are on the other side of forgiveness and fear. There is nothing to fear. Do it with authority and with confidence that God has your back and has not forgotten you or forsaken you – ever!

Chapter Thirteen

Seven Steps to a Healed Heart

Philippians 4:13
***13** I can do all this through him who gives me strength.*

Many of you may think, "I want to forgive and I want to heal, but how do I start? Where do I begin? What if I am wasting my time? I don't think our relationship can be saved," and so on and so forth. Don't let the enemy play with your head or emotions. The following steps can be used as a guide in your own personal journey of forgiveness and healing. Take it one day at a time.

1. ***Pray for God's strength to overcome deep-rooted hurt.*** Initially, you may be angry with God for what happened. It may take you

time to muster the strength to pray, but it is necessary that you pray.

2. ***Confront the father/mother (or person) who hurt you, after things have cooled off, in a respectful manner***. Perhaps it has been years since you last spoke. You must be tactful when you have a face-to-face moment. I would not advise you to take that step of mending the relationship via text, email, or snail mail. This requires one-on-one interaction. You can do it! You must do it! And you will do it!

3. ***Choose to forgive and realize it will take time to gain the strength to do so***. There is so much healing power when we decide to forgive those who have hurt us. You will benefit the most when you forgive. There is **freedom** when you forgive.

4. ***Do yourself a favor – and forgive!*** It will bring peace of mind and soul and healing to your body. Holding on to grudges will affect your health. It's not worth putting your health at risk, because at the end of the day, whether or not you get an apology

from the person/s who hurt you, you help yourself when you forgive.

5. ***Vent as much as possible, grieve, cry, and get it out your system***! There must be a mourning/ grieving process because we are emotional creatures. Give yourself as much time as you need to grieve. Don't let anyone tell you, "Get over it," or "It's time to move on" – you are the only person who can determine when it's time to move on. Do not let society or people's opinions dictate the time you need to process things.

6. ***If needed, particularly if you have trust issues, seek counseling for as long as it takes.*** Make sure you find a good fit of a counselor to address your specific needs. If you desire marriage, counseling isn't a choice but a **must** before you go into a committed relationship. Trust and loyalty, and lack thereof, can make or break a relationship.

7. ***Allow time to fully heal your wounds.*** As time progresses and healing has taken place, try to establish and/or mend your father/

daughter relationship. If that is not at all possible, go into your private room with the Lord and hash it out with Him; bring it **_ALL_** to the cross and leave it there! He will make it happen in its own time.

Chapter Fourteen

Scriptures of Forgiveness

Matthew 18:21-22

21 Then Peter came to Jesus and asked, "Lord, how many times shall I forgive my brother or sister who sins against me? Up to seven times?"

22 Jesus answered, "I tell you, not seven times, but seventy-seven times."

Mark 11:25

25 And when you stand praying, if you hold anything against anyone, forgive them, so that your Father in heaven may forgive you your sins.

Luke 17:3

3 So watch yourselves.

"If your brother or sister sins against you, rebuke them; and if they repent, forgive them."

Luke 6:37
37 Do not judge, and you will not be judged. Do not condemn, and you will not be condemned. Forgive, and you will be forgiven.

Ephesians 4:32
32 Be kind and compassionate to one another, forgiving each other, just as in Christ God forgave you.

EPILOGUE

Hi guys, I'm Jorge, Rosa's younger brother by three years. Let me start by saying I feel honored and blessed to have been asked to be a part of this book and to have such a wonderful, talented, and loving sister. Rosa is a strong force in my life, and I couldn't have gotten through many obstacles without her by my side. Rosa has always been my fierce defender, and although we sometimes fight and argue, I always feel loved by her. I thank God my sister has such great morals that she lives by. I can only hope that my faith will be at the level that hers is with our Heavenly Father.

Speaking of fathers, I don't have the same close relationship with our father that Rosa has. But having read this book, I have had a revelation – my father is only human. He made huge mistakes as a father, but just as parents forgive their children for mistakes they make, we as children should also forgive and honor our fathers and mothers.

This is something I had not done with my father, but it is something I will need to do in time. To speak the words, "Dad, I forgive you and I love you!" You see, I saw my father as a distant uncle as far as my relationship with him was concerned. He was never around, and I don't ever remember having a truly loving, affectionate relationship with him. He has grown on me through the years, but it is still hard for me to communicate with him. It is sad to say, but his infidelity toward my mother really affected me negatively. At one point, I despised him so much that I just felt a cold, bitter hole in my heart for him. I couldn't have cared less about him, and he was just an insert-father-here figure; anyone could have filled that slot.

Reading and digesting this book, I have come to find out I didn't know of a lot of things that were hidden from me. Rosa has shared things I had no clue ever happened. I'm a little resentful at the relationship she and my father have now. I used to think, "Why does she love and care for this man so much?" He was useless as a father, although he provided for us financially. I just couldn't see what the closeness between them was all about. But now I understand

Epilogue

why Rosa has such affection and love for our father; she forgave him wholeheartedly.

It's great to see the new person who is my sister, Rosa. She is less angry, less judgmental, and less selfish. Rosa is now wiser, selfless, and more of service. She has no idea what impact her character as a person has on my life, and on many others who watch her every move. It is truly a blessing to have a sister who has overcome the "betrayal by a father" and who has been able to deal with the problem head-on with the help of God and others who have come into contact with her.

I have also learned to forgive my father for what he did to our family; after all, he's only human. My father is truly a blessing for me now that he is retired and has time for his children. I can see now that he is a caring father who is and was only trying to do his best with the character defects he has, probably pasted on by what he learned growing up. It wasn't his fault; it is all he knew about parenting. But at least there is love and kindness in his heart for me and our family. He sometimes tells me, "I just want the best for you guys! What father wouldn't want the best for his children!"

I look forward to the stories and life experiences he so eagerly loves to share in our hair salon on the days when he comes into work. He loves to go on about how he worked seven days a week, taking an English course three nights a week for four hours per night; coming home after 10 p.m. hungry and tired. "I did it for my family, because I wanted the best for my children!" is what he tells everyone. I know my father wasn't always there for me emotionally, but he was there always. I remember as a child, I would request to sleep by his side because I loved to bear hug him and fall asleep in his arms. In the morning, he would no longer be by my side, and I would sometimes cry hysterically because he had abandoned me in the middle of the night. Loving my dad now is so different from when I was a child; it is the kind of love that admires, esteems, and is completely unconditional!

I want to end on this: forgiveness is required to live a joyous life. Forgiveness, I realize now, can mend hearts, restore broken homes, and unite families. Forgiving those who hurt or abandoned us, and forgiving ourselves for the trauma we endured at the hands of those who inflicted it. People are people, not saints, and definitely not perfect beings, so we must remember the one who is greater than us all, who forgave us for all of our earthly sins! Jesus is His name. Thank you, and I hope that you enjoy this book and truly learn that the power of forgiveness can be a great blessing!